Why can't I...
roar like a lion?

and other questions
about sound

Sally Hewitt

Belitha Press

First published in the UK in 2002 by
Belitha Press
A member of Chrysalis Books plc
64 Brewery Road, London N7 9NT

ISBN 1 84138 445 3

British Library Cataloguing in Publication Data
for this book is available from the British Library.

Series editor: Jean Coppendale
Designer: Jacqueline Palmer and Fanny Level
Picture researcher: Terry Forshaw, Louise Daubeny and Jenny Barlow
Consultant: Helen Walters
Face painting: Julie Clark – Magic Faces

Printed in Hong Kong

10 9 8 7 6 5 4 3 2 1

Picture acknowledgements:
(T) = Top, (B) = Bottom, (L) = Left, (R) = Right, (B/G) = Background,
(C) = Centre

Front Cover (B/G) Chrysalis Images; 3 (TL), 7 inset & 30 (T) Chrysalis Images; 3
(TC) & 21 (T) © M. Watson/Ardea; 3 (TR), 12 (TR) (BR) & 28 © John
Bracegirdle/Wild Images/RSPCA Photolibrary; 8-9 T (B/G) © Yoji Hirose/Galaxy
Picture Library, B (B/G) © NASA; 10 (B/G) © Stephen Frink/Corbis; 11 (T) &
(CR) Chrysalis Images; 12 inset © Lynda Richardson/Corbis; 13 (R) © Robert &
Linda Mostyn; Eye Ubiquitous/Corbis; 14 (B/G) Digital Vision; 16 (B/G) © Kevin
R. Morris/Corbis; 17 (B/G) © Tony Arruza/Corbis; 20 (L) & 30 (B) © Angela
Hampton/RSPCAPhotolibrary; 23 inset © Emanuel Maria/RSPCA Photolibrary;
26 inset © Colin Cradock, Wild Images Ltd/RSPCA Photolibrary.

All other photography Ray Moller.

Contents

The world is full of sounds. Even when it seems quiet you can probably hear something.

What can you hear now?
Can you hear an aeroplane flying overhead?
Is someone talking nearby?
Is the radio on?

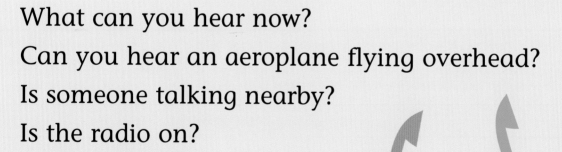

Sounds are made when something moves.

Something that is perfectly still doesn't make a sound.

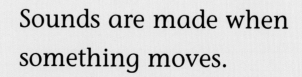

Hearing sounds helps you to know what is going on around you.

If you shut your eyes, you can still tell if a tap is running or that someone is running up the stairs by the sounds that they make.

But what is sound?

This book will explain that sound is invisible, that there are no sounds in space and that however careful you are, you cannot move silently.

Why can't I switch off my ears?

Because your ears are made for hearing sounds all the time.

When something makes a sound it moves the air around it. The moving air goes into your ears and you hear the sound.

You can block your ears to keep sound out, but you can't switch them off.

Why have I got drums in my ears?

Because you couldn't hear without your **eardrums**.

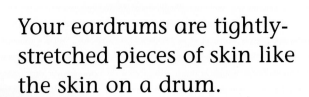

Your eardrums are tightly-stretched pieces of skin like the skin on a drum.

When a sound hits them, they **vibrate** or move very fast.

The **vibrations** send messages to your brain, which tells you what you are hearing.

Sound is made by moving air that travels in **sound waves**.

There is no air in **space** to carry sound waves so without air, there is no sound.

It is very quiet in space.

Astronauts wear spacesuits and carry air to breathe. They talk to each other by radio.

Why can I hear under water?

Because sound can travel through water.

You can hear dolphins calling to each other as their voices send sound waves through the water.

Sound needs something to travel through. You can hear sound travelling through metal, the ground and even through walls.

Why can I hear the sea in a shell?

Because air moving inside a shell sounds like the sea.

Empty tubes coil round and round inside some shells.

As air moves around the tubes it makes a noise.

If you put the shell to your ear you hear the air moving.

Why can't I move about silently?

Because when you move about you make the air around you move.

You can't move about without touching something and making sound waves.

The only things that are **silent** are perfectly still.

A cat can creep through the grass and hardly make a sound.

Why do loud sounds hurt my ears?

Because loud sounds make stronger vibrations than quiet sounds.

Sound waves vibrate tiny bones and the eardrums inside your ears, so very loud sounds can hurt your ears.

People who work with noisy machines wear earmuffs to protect their ears.

13

Why can I see and not hear my friends?

Because the further away you are from a sound, the quieter it becomes.

As sound travels through the air, it spreads out and becomes fainter and fainter.

When you stand near your friends you can hear their voices loudly.

You can hardly hear them from far away.

How can my voice travel without me?

Because your voice can travel along wires and through the air.

When you talk on the telephone, your voice is changed into electric signals which travel along wires to the person you are talking to.

Mobile phones send your voice through the air along **radio waves** that you can't see.

Why can't I talk to my echo?

Because your **echo** can only repeat what you say.

You hear an echo when you shout at a wall or a cliff some distance away from you.

The sound bounces back and you hear your voice again.

Why does the wind howl?

Because wind makes a noise when it blows through small spaces.

Wind gets everywhere. It shakes the branches of trees and makes the air vibrate along pipes and in the gaps between buildings.

The vibrating air makes a howling sound like a giant wind instrument.

Why do instruments make different sounds?

Because they are different shapes and you play them in different ways.

A guitar is a **stringed instrument**. You pluck or strum the strings to make them vibrate and play notes.

A drum is a **percussion instrument**. The drum skin vibrates and makes a sound when you hit it.

A recorder and a trumpet are both **wind instruments**. When you blow into them, the air inside them vibrates and you hear a note.

Why can't I hear as well as my dog?

Because your dog has big ears for collecting sounds.

The part of the your ear that you can see is called your earflap.

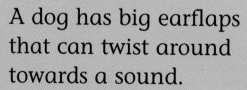

A dog has big earflaps that can twist around towards a sound.

A dog needs to hear very well to hunt for food and listen out for danger.

20

Why can't I hear a bat squeak?

Because a bat squeak is too high for your ears to hear.

A bat squeaks to find food in the dark.

The sound of the squeaks hit a juicy moth and bounce back like an echo.

The bat hears the echo and knows exactly where to find the moth.

Why can't I roar like a lion?

Because your voice box is too small.

The lump in your throat is your voice box. Flaps in your voice box called **vocal chords** make sounds when air vibrates them.

Longer vocal chords make deeper sounds than shorter ones.

A lion has a big voice box and long vocal chords, so his roar is deep and very loud.

Why can't I see sound?

Because sound is **invisible**.

You can see what makes a sound but you can't actually see the sound it makes.

If you shut your eyes, you can tell what is happening around you by the sounds that you hear.

Why can't I catch sound?

Because you can only feel vibrations made by sound, you can't hold it.

You can keep sound by **recording** it.

Sound can be recorded onto tapes and CDs which you can listen to again and again.

Why does lightning flash...

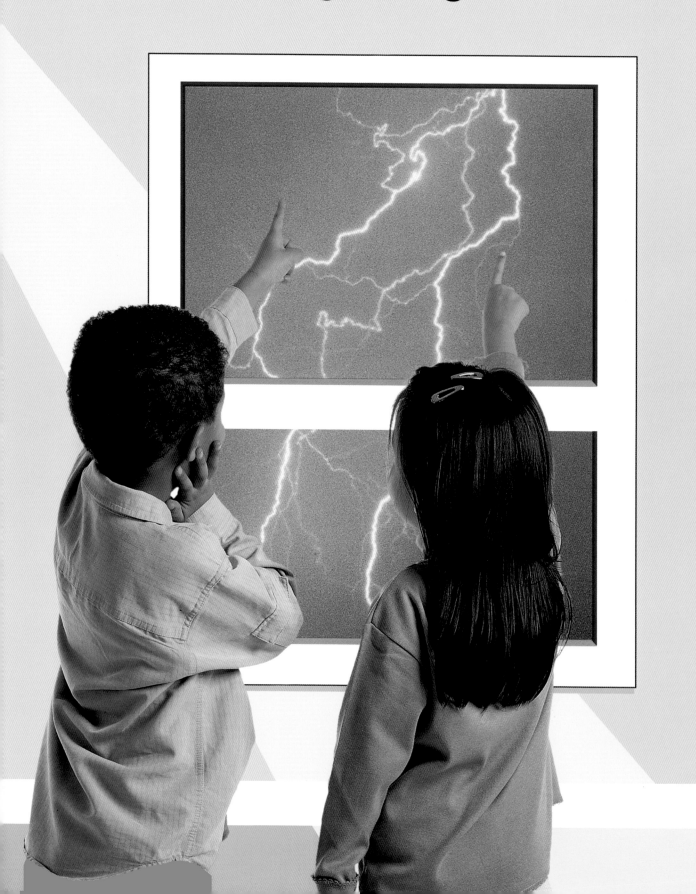

...before thunder crashes?

Because light travels faster than sound.

Thunder and lightning happen at exactly the same time.

You see the lightning flash first because light travels faster than anything else in the universe.

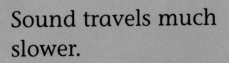

Sound travels much slower.

If a storm is several kilometres away from you, you will hear thunder a few seconds after you see lightning.

27

Sound words

eardrums Eardrums are in the part of your ears inside your head. They are tightly stretched pieces of skin. They vibrate when a sound hits them and you hear that sound.

echo When a sound such as your voice hits something such as a wall, it bounces back towards you and you hear the sound again. This is called an echo.

invisible When something is invisible, it is there but you can't see it. Sound is invisible. You can hear it but you can't see it.

percussion instrument A percussion instrument is a musical instrument that you play by hitting or rattling it to make a note or a sound. Drums and triangles are percussion instruments.

radio waves Radio waves are invisible waves all around us that can carry sounds and pictures through the air and through space.

recording When you make a recording you capture sounds or pictures on discs or tapes so you can watch or listen to them over and over again.

sound waves A sound wave is made when something moves and vibrates the air around it. Sound travels in waves through air, water or solid things such as the ground.

space We call the enormous empty places between the stars and planets space. There is no sound in space because there is no air there.

stringed instrument A stringed instrument is a musical instrument that you play by plucking, strumming or scraping the strings to make them vibrate. A guitar and a violin are stringed instruments.

vibrate Vibrate means to move a tiny distance very quickly to and fro.

vibrations Vibrations are tiny movements made by a sound. You can feel vibrations if you touch a drum or a guitar when they are played.

vocal chords Vocal chords are flaps in your voice box, in your throat, that vibrate to make the sound of your voice.

wind instrument A wind instrument is a musical instrument you play by blowing into it. A flute and a recorder are wind instruments.

Activities

Try to hear in your head the sounds that all these things make. Sort them into loud and quiet sounds. They may be quiet sometimes and loud at other times.

- thunder
- a running tap
- a bird singing
- an aeroplane
- a train
- a bicycle

- a piano
- a kettle boiling
- breathing
- singing
- a bee
- the wind

Match the things below to one or more words that describe the sound they make.

traffic   rain

washing up

thunder
          a bell

leaves in the wind

clatter   rustle

rumble

clang

splash

crash

Notes for parents and teachers

Children know that they cannot see sound, but they may not know the reason why. Spend some time together thinking about the questions in this book and the possibilities they raise before reading the simple, factual answers. You may like to try out these activities with your child. They will reinforce what you have learned about sound and give you plenty to talk about.

Listen!

Sit with your child, shut your eyes, stay very still and listen for about two minutes. Open your eyes and tell each other what you heard. Did you both hear the same things? Did you know what made all the sounds that you heard?

Earflaps

Rabbits and dogs, and many other animals can swivel their ears towards a sound. Cup your hand behind one of your ears to make the earflap bigger. Now point your cupped ear towards a very faint sound such as a computer humming or a radio turned down low. Can you hear it louder and clearer?

Guess the sound

Ask your child to shut his or her eyes and listen to some sounds that you make. Can they guess what you are doing? Writing with a pencil, opening a can of fizzy drink, pouring milk, yawning, undoing a zip and opening a drawer are just a few things that make interesting sounds.

Make a telephone

Make a hole in the bottom of two plastic cups. Thread a long piece of string through the holes and attach buttons to each end to keep the string in place. Stretch the string tight. Speak into one cup while your child puts the other cup to his or her ear and listens. Swap over and have a chat on the phone!

Index